Mom & Dad,

Tell Me
Your Story

Precious memories,
invaluable wisdom and
personal experience
for your children

Dear Mom, dear Dad!

You have already experienced a lot. Did great things, had a lot of fun and went through thick and thin together.

With all the lightness and joy you have always increased in wisdom, gathered experiences and have been profoundly shaped.

Of course, there were also moments in your life when the warm sunlight hid behind dark clouds. Where you were not so well.

All these stories and experiences from life are a precious treasure for your children.

It would be too bad if we never heard this abundance of stories and happenings.

Also, you surely have a lot of advice and recommendations how we can behave optimally in different circumstances.

We want you to take the time to look at your life.

With this book you get a selection of far-reaching questions that you can answer. Your answers will enrich us and give us even more insights into your life.

We hope you enjoy the writing!

With great love,

Childhood

Mom as
a child

Dad as
a child

Childhood

How did your parents find each other?

Under what circumstances did your birth take place?

Do your first names have a deeper meaning?

Childhood

Are you happy with your first names?

Do you have siblings?

How was the relationship and harmony in your family?

Childhood

Do you have nicknames?

"Every child is an artist.
The problem is how to
remain an artist once we
grow up."

Pablo Picasso

What's the first thing that comes to mind when you think of your childhood?

Childhood

What made your kids' eyes light up?

_____

_____

_____

_____

Were you rich?

_____

_____

_____

_____

What was the house/apartment like where you grew up?

_____

_____

_____

_____

_____

Moms
home

Dads
home

Childhood

What neighborhood did you live in?

_____

_____

_____

_____

_____

How did you learn to ride a bike?

_____

_____

_____

_____

_____

How did you do in school?

_____

_____

_____

_____

_____

Childhood

Do you still have childhood friends today?

_____

_____

_____

_____

_____

What stories did you like to hear?

_____

_____

_____

_____

_____

Did you have animals?

_____

_____

_____

_____

_____

What profession did you dream of at that time?

_____

_____

_____

_____

"The soul is healed by being with children."

Fyodor Dostoevsky

Where did you go most often on vacation?

_____

_____

_____

_____

Childhood

What was your favorite dish that your parents/grandparents made?

Did you get hurt as a child? How did it happen?

What impactful or drastic life experience did you have as a child?

Childhood

Did you have fears? Do they still exist today?

_____

_____

_____

_____

_____

What activity as a child would you still like to do today?

_____

_____

_____

_____

_____

Favorite games as a child

01 ....

02 ....

03 ....

04 ....

05 ....

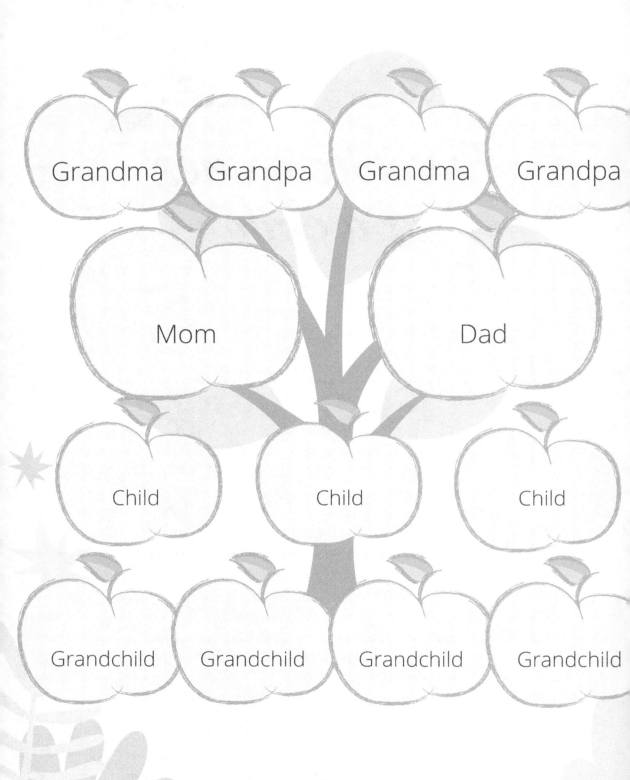

Puberty

Mom as
a teen

Dad as
a teen

Puberty

How did you dress?

_____

_____

_____

_____

_____

Do you have a special characteristic of your body that makes you stand out?

_____

_____

_____

_____

Do you look more like your mother or father?

_____

_____

_____

_____

Puberty

What memory from your youth still brings you laughter today?

_____

_____

_____

_____

What problems did you have to deal with?

_____

_____

_____

_____

_____

What characteristics of your parents were you determined *not* to adopt?

_____

_____

_____

_____

What was your attitude towards the teachers like?

_____
_____
_____
_____
_____

"Puberty is a potpourri of emotions."

Marina Zuber

Did you enjoy going to school?

_____
_____
_____
_____
_____

Puberty

Have you committed any crimes?

_____

_____

_____

_____

_____

What political/cultural events took place when you were a teen?

_____

_____

_____

_____

Which stars did you admire?

_____

_____

_____

_____

Puberty

What did you learn in class that you remember very well today?

_____

_____

_____

_____

What did you think about old people?

_____

_____

_____

_____

What was the craziest thing you did as a teenager?

_____

_____

_____

_____

What were your best vacations as a teenager?

_____

_____

_____

_____

"Youth is the gift of nature, but age is a work of art."

Stanislaw Jerzy
Lec

What terribly embarrassing thing happened to you?

_____

_____

_____

_____

Puberty

Were you envious of the lives of others around you?

_____

_____

_____

_____

What hobbies did you have?

_____

_____

_____

_____

Have you participated in any contests?

_____

_____

_____

_____

THAT SHAPED OUR
GENERATION

1

2

3

4

5

6

7

8

9

10

Adulthood

Mom as
an adult

Dad as
an adult

Why I'm so grateful to have you two:

I have a great example to follow. You!

You always have the right words to make everything more pleasant.

Nothing is better than the love of parents, and the same can be said about you.

You give the most amazing hugs!

You are the most wonderful Mom & Dad in this world!

Adulthood

What did you love to do as adults?

_____

_____

_____

_____

_____

What are you grateful for?

_____

_____

_____

_____

_____

Does a song have a special meaning for you?

_____

_____

_____

_____

_____

Adulthood

Have you taken to the streets for social interests?

_____

_____

_____

_____

_____

What is the best compliment you have received?

_____

_____

_____

_____

_____

What was your first car?

_____

_____

_____

_____

_____

_____

Your first car

What approach to finances have you cultivated?

"Yesterday is history, tomorrow is a mystery, today is a gift of God, which is why we call it the present."

Bil Keane

What was your biggest bad buy?

How resilient were you under stress?

_____

_____

_____

_____

_____

How did you two meet?

_____

_____

_____

_____

_____

When did you move in together?

_____

_____

_____

_____

_____

Adulthood

From Mom: "What I appreciate about Dad"

Adulthood

From Dad: "What I appreciate about Mom"

Adulthood

How was your wedding?

Do any of you snore?

At what age did you become parents?

To Mom: What was it like for you to be pregnant?

_____

_____

_____

_____

_____

"There shall be an eternal summer in the grateful heart."

Celia Thaxter

How did you choose your children's names?

_____

_____

_____

_____

_____

Adulthood

Where did you learn about raising children?

_____

_____

_____

_____

_____

What is the most wonderful thing about being a parent?

_____

_____

_____

_____

How has being a parent shaped you personally?

_____

_____

_____

_____

_____

What outrageous things did your children do?

What were the funniest things your children did?

Which of your children's first words can you remember?

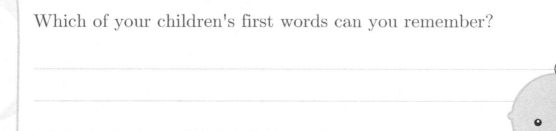

Adulthood

What are you proud of regarding your children?

Have you traveled a lot? Tell me about your most beautiful journey together!

Have you met any famous people?

Important cities for us:

Adulthood

Important countries for us:

What unexplainable phenomena / supernatural miracles have you experienced?

_____

_____

_____

_____

_____

What makes you smile?

_____

_____

_____

_____

What important life wisdom would you share with your "18-year-old self"?

_____

_____

_____

_____

TOP 10
mistakes to avoid

1

2

3

4

5

6

7

8

9

10

*He achieved success who has lived well,
laughed often, and loved much;*

*Who has enjoyed the trust of pure women,
the respect of intelligent men and
the love of little children;*

Who has filled his niche and accomplished his task;

*Who has never lacked appreciation of Earth's beauty
or failed to express it;*

*Who has left the world better than he found it,
Whether an improved poppy, a perfect poem,
or a rescued soul;*

*Who has always looked for the best in others and
given them the best he had;*

Whose life was an inspiration;

Whose memory a benediction.

Bessie Anderson Stanley, 1897-1952

Higher
Age

Mom
today

Dad
today

Higher Age

How did you get to your current house/apartment?

What are you most looking forward to about (future) retirement?

Is it hard to get older?

Do you regret (not) doing something?

Do you have a "skeleton in the closet"?

What do you do all day long?

WELLNESS-DAY

Choose an activity for your self-care and have a feel-good day.

Do sports

Drink tea

Go for a walk

Do something creative

Read a book

Listen to music

What topics do you like to talk about?

"Age does not protect you from love, but love protects you from age."

Jeanne Moreau

What would your perfect day look like?

Higher Age

What is the best memory of your life as a couple so far?

_____

_____

_____

_____

How do you look at youth now?

_____

_____

_____

_____

What do you not dare to tell the children personally in conversation?

_____

_____

_____

_____

Higher Age

If you had one wish: What would you wish for?

_____

_____

_____

_____

Do you feel lonely?

_____

_____

_____

_____

_____

What has your opinion changed radically compared to before?

_____

_____

_____

_____

OUR FAVORITE PRODUCTS IN THE SUPERMARKET:

How has your character changed?

What would you rescue from a burning house?

Are you afraid of dying?

THINGS THAT YOU UNDERSTAND WHEN YOU'RE OLDER

Staying at home is also fun	Things will develop as they should	Relationships are everything	It's perfectly ok, to be vulnerable	pay bills on time
"I should have saved more money!"	Work is not everything	Visit the family more often	Always trust your intuition	Success does not happen overnight
Efforts are part of life	There is always something new to learn about life	Don't take it so seriously	Getting out of your comfort zone is important	There are no ordinary Moments
Better late than never	Relax more often	To realize the desired life is beautiful	Health is wealth	You are never too old to learn something new
Time heals all wounds	Thank people more	Talking is the best therapy	Your mistakes do not define you	8 hours of sleep is pure bliss

Higher Age

Do you believe in life after death?

If you believe in it: How do you get to heaven?

What are your aspirations for your funeral?

Does a certain smell evoke intense memories in you?

_____

_____

_____

_____

_____

"Gray hair is a crown of splendor; it is attained in the way of righteousness."

Proverbs 16:31

Do you want to move/emigrate?

_____

_____

_____

_____

_____

Higher Age

What goals and dreams do you have for the future?

_____

_____

_____

_____

_____

Was everything better in the past?

_____

_____

_____

_____

_____

What moments in life are you especially happy about?

_____

_____

_____

_____

_____

Higher Age

From which life crisis did you emerge stronger?

Which people have helped you in a special way?

What important experiences would you like to share?

Higher Age

What can I do to delight you?

_____
_____
_____
_____

How do you imagine the world in 2050?

_____
_____
_____
_____

What is your life so far in one sentence?

_____
_____
_____
_____

Goals for the future

For my parents!

These lines are for you -
for my parents, whom I love.

You took care of me for years,
but did rarely hear how much you mean to me.
I would therefore like to take this opportunity to say
thank you.

You have helped me from the beginning,
when I took the first, wobbly steps and
are still there for me today, when I fall down some time.

Thank you for letting me go a little more with each step,
so I could learn to stand on my own two feet.
Thank you that I could always feel safe with you.
Thank you for the love I could always be sure of.

Thank you for the many years in which you have never
stopped
to care for me and in whom you have tried everything,
to turn my dreams into successes.

Thank you for your patience and understanding,
That you gave me when I went my own way.
Thank you for your love, without which I could not have lived.
Thank you for everything you have done and are still doing for
me!

With your love and experience you have made me that person,
who I am today.

Hopefully I will be able to give my children
as much as you've given to me.

Relationships

Relationships

What do you admire about your parents?

What caused conflicts with your parents?

Is there love at first sight?

Relationships

How did you overcome the first heartbreak?

_____

_____

_____

_____

_____

How did you know mom/dad was the one?

_____

_____

_____

_____

_____

What are the requirements for marriage?

_____

_____

_____

_____

_____

How to get along well with the in-laws?

"Darkness cannot drive out darkness; only light can do that. Hate cannot drive out hate; only love can do that."

Martin Luther King, Jr.

Can you remember your first dispute?

Relationships

What advice do you have for a beautiful marriage?

_____

_____

_____

_____

_____

How do you find the relationship today in our family?

_____

_____

_____

_____

_____

What advice do you have for successful parenting?

_____

_____

_____

_____

Pet names to mom

Pet names to dad

What attributes of people make you angry?

How do you learn forgiveness?

How do you deal with criticism?

When was the last time you said "I love you!" to someone?

_____

_____

_____

"A drop of love is more than an ocean of knowledge."

Blaise Pascal

What do you appreciate most about other people?

_____

_____

_____

_____

Relationships

Why do others seek your presence?

_____
_____
_____
_____
_____

What puts others off from you?

_____
_____
_____
_____
_____

Who are your friends today?

_____
_____
_____
_____
_____

How have you dealt with bereavement?

How do you want others to remember you?

How do you define love?

TOP 10 RULES
Dealing with people

1

2

3

4

5

6

7

8

9

10

Career

Career

Should there be mandatory community service?

What vocational training/studies have you completed?

What was/is your favorite job?

Career

What kind of work can you not stand at all?

Have you ever failed with your own business?

Which of your work activities would you do without pay?

How do you make decisions?

"I can't change the direction of the wind, but I can adjust my sails to always reach my destination."

Jimmy Dean

How to find the dream job?

DO YOU HAVE SLEEP PROBLEMS?

TRY THESE TIPS!

1. No distractions in your room

2. No coffee or sweet drinks 5 hours before bedtime

3. Exercise regularly

4. Too many thoughts? Write them down in a journal.

5. If you can't sleep, don't force it.

6. If your lack of sleep is affecting your daily life, consult a doctor.

Career

Which boss do you think back to with favor?

_____

_____

_____

_____

Have you found the meaning of life after all these years?

_____

_____

_____

_____

For which problem of mankind would you like to have a solution?

_____

_____

_____

_____

Career

What topic would you like to write a book about?

_____

_____

_____

_____

Whose heroic work would you like to have made?
(Example: Martin Luther King, Jr.)

_____

_____

_____

What superhero power would you like to have?

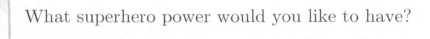

_____

_____

_____

_____

Career

Do you do any volunteer work?

"Pleasure in the job puts perfection in the work."

Aristotle

For which organization / project could I donate?

Tips for career success

01 ....

02 ....

03 ....

04 ....

05 ....

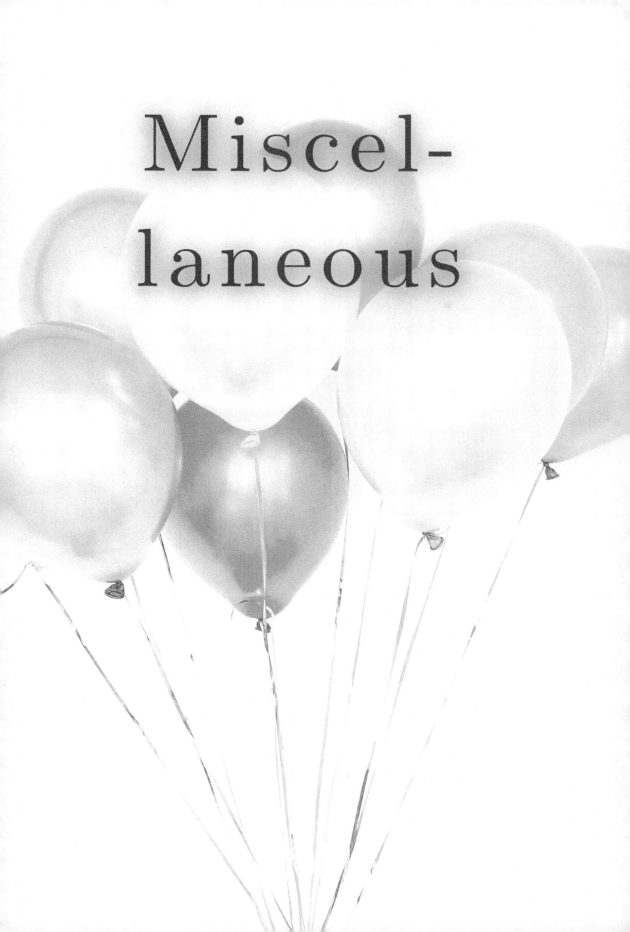

Miscel-
laneous

This or that

Which do you prefer?

(Please mark: Mom's color | Dad's color)

City trip	Beach
Relaxed	Nervous
Save	Waste
Meat	Vegetables
Stubborn	Harmonious
Vanilla	Chocolate
Comedy	Action
Elevator	Stairs
Classic	Hip Hop
Cinema	Couch

This or that

Which do you prefer?

Jogging	Volleyball
Family	Career
Introvert	Extrovert
Summer	Winter
Conscientious	Sloppy
Coffee	Tea
Conservative	Liberal
Left	Right
Sleep in	Early Bird
Dog	Cat

This or that

Which do you prefer?

Pajamas	Tuxedo
Garden	Roof terrace
Flying	Taking a train
Optimistic	Pessimistic
Party	Chilling
Nutella	Honey
Teamwork	Alone
Sweden	Spain
Farm	Villa
Email	Call

This or that

Which do you prefer?

Whole milk	Bittersweet
Inside young	Old & wise
Cooking	Delivery service
Swimming pool	Lake
Colorful	Grey
Apple	Samsung
Long hair	Short hair
Bicycle	Car
Heart	Head
Slippers	High Heels

This or that

Which do you prefer?

Makeup	Nature
Kitchen	Living room
World hunger	Climate change
Sweet	Salty
Watching sports	Doing sports
Cash	Bitcoin
Flea Market	Shopping Mall
Home Office	Business Trip
Economics	Philosophy
YouTube	Podcast

This or that

Which do you prefer?

Freezing	Sweating
1900	2100
Rice	Noodles
Amazon	Kiosk
Chess	Uno
Sun	Moon
Paperback	eBook
Money	Fame
Office	Garage
Gifts	Compliments

TOP 10
Wisdoms of life

1

2

3

4

5

6

7

8

9

10

Favorite books

01 ....

02 ....

03 ....

04 ....

05 ....

Our favorite spots

Favorite words

1

2

3

4

5

6

7

8

9

10

Favorite websites

Own questions

Letter from mom

Letter from mom

Letter from dad

Letter from dad

Space for other content

Space for other content

Space for other content

Made in the USA
Las Vegas, NV
09 May 2024

89709347R00063